Prime Ministers of Canada

The New Nation

By Bev Cline

Weigl

CALGARY
www.weigl.com

Published by Weigl Educational Publishers Limited
6325 10 Street SE
Calgary, Alberta, Canada
T2H 2Z9

Website: www.weigl.com

Library and Archives Canada Cataloguing in Publication

Cline, Beverly Fink, 1951-
      The new nation / Beverly Cline.
(Prime ministers of Canada)
Includes index.
ISBN 1-55388-247-4 (bound).--ISBN 1-55388-246-6 (pbk.)
      1. Prime ministers--Canada--Biography--Juvenile literature.
2. Canada--History--1867-1914--Juvenile literature. I. Title.
II. Series: Prime ministers of Canada (Calgary, Alta.)
FC26.P7C63 2006   j971.009'9   C2006-902474-X

Printed in Canada
1 2 3 4 5 6 7 8 9 0 10 09 08 07 06

Cover: Canada's first prime minister, Sir John A. Macdonald, was born in 1815.

Photo Credits: Glenbow Museum Archives: pages 5 (nc-6-11899), 21 (NA_3173-9), 22 (NA-494-18), 36 (NA-1406-218); **Library and Archives Canada:** pages 1 (C-021597), 4 (C-005327, C-010460, PA-033933, C-001971), 5 (C-00687, PA-128175), 12 (C-3918), 19 (C-31264), 26 (C-021597), 28 (C-010460, C-000698, RD002067), 29 (C-002829), 30 (C-0104600, 38 (RD002067); **Saskatchewan Archives:** pages 4 (R-D700), 23 (R-B 3809), 28 (R-D700), 32 (RD-700), 34 (RD-700).

We acknowledge the financial support of the Government of Canada through the Book Publishing Industry Development Program (BPIDP) for our publishing activities.

Project Coordinator
Tatiana Tomljanovic

Design
Terry Paulhus

All of the Internet URLs given in the book were valid at the time of publication. However, due to the dynamic nature of the Internet, some addresses may have changed, or sites may have ceased to exist since publication. While the author and publisher regret any inconvenience this may cause readers, no responsibility for any such changes can be accepted by either the author or the publisher.

Contents

Canada's Prime Ministers

Since **Confederation**, there have been 22 Canadian prime ministers. Canada's prime ministers have come from many provinces and cultures. Some of them, such as the first prime minister, John A. Macdonald, were born in other countries. They came to Canada because they, or their parents, decided Canada was the best place to live and raise a family.

Canada's prime ministers are people of many talents and different interests. Some trained as lawyers, while others were journalists, doctors, farmers, writers, teachers, business people, and members of the **civil service**. Some of them fought as soldiers to protect Canada and her allies. All of them had one thing in common. They wanted to make Canada one of the best places in the world to live.

THE NEW NATION (CONFEDERATION TO 1896)

John A. Macdonald
(July 1, 1867–November 5, 1873; October 17, 1878–June 6, 1891)

Alexander Mackenzie
(November 7, 1873–October 8, 1878)

John J. C. Abbott
(June 16, 1891–November 24, 1892)

John S. D. Thompson
(December 5, 1892–December 12, 1894)

Mackenzie Bowell
(December 21, 1894–April 27, 1896)

Charles H. Tupper
(May 1, 1896–July 8, 1896)

TURN OF THE 20TH CENTURY (1896–1920)

Wilfrid Laurier
(July 11, 1896–October 6, 1911)

Robert L. Borden
(October 10, 1911–July 10, 1920)

TIME OF TURMOIL (1920–1948)

Arthur Meighen
(July 10, 1920–December 29, 1921; June 29, 1926–September 25, 1926)

Richard B. Bennett
(August 7, 1930–October 23, 1935)

William Lyon Mackenzie King
(December 29, 1921–June 28, 1926; September 25, 1926–August 7, 1930; October 23, 1935–November 15, 1948)

TIME OF TRANSITION (1948–1968)

TRUDEAU ERA (1968–1984)

Louis S. Saint Laurent
(November 15, 1948–June 21, 1957)

John George Diefenbaker
(June 21, 1957–April 22, 1963)

Lester B. Pearson
(April 22, 1963–April 20, 1968)

Pierre Elliott Trudeau
(April 20, 1968–June 3, 1979; March 3, 1980–June 30, 1984)

Charles Joseph Clark
(June 4, 1979–March 2, 1980)

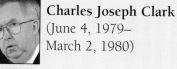

John N. Turner
(June 30, 1984–September 17, 1984)

CONTEMPORARY CANADA (1984 TO PRESENT)

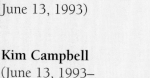

Martin Brian Mulroney
(September 17, 1984–June 13, 1993)

Jean J. Chrétien
(October 25, 1993–December 12, 2003)

Kim Campbell
(June 13, 1993–October 25, 1993)

Paul E. P. Martin
(December 12, 2003–February 6, 2006)

Stephen J. Harper
(February 6, 2006–)

John A. Macdonald: Canada's First Prime Minister

Sir John A. Macdonald has been called the "Chief Architect of Canada" because of his role in Canada's early political development.

Many people believe that January 11th should be a national holiday. It was on this day in 1815 that John Alexander Macdonald was born.

Macdonald accomplished many goals in his lifetime. As an adult, he founded a new country called Canada. He became the first prime minister of Canada and led the country for more than 19 years. He was also knighted by the Queen of England and became known as "Sir John."

Macdonald became one of Canada's most important politicians. He is remembered for being a Father of Confederation.

Macdonald made laws that affect Canadians today. He was responsible for the creation of the Canadian Pacific Railway (CPR), which united the country from east to west and established the Royal Canadian Mounted Police. Yet, Macdonald still found time to stop in the street to talk to children. He would take off his familiar tall, black silk hat so it would not fall off onto the muddy, unpaved streets. Then he would stoop down and play a game of marbles.

Black silk top hats were a fashionable accessory for men during the late 19th century.

Keeping Canada Together

"The place of Sir John A. Macdonald in this country was so large and so absorbing that it is almost impossible to conceive that the politics of this country—the fate of this country—will continue without him… It may be said without any exaggeration whatever, that the life of Sir John Macdonald, from the time he entered **Parliament**, is the history of Canada."

*Wilfrid Laurier, the **House of Commons**, June 8, 1891*

Growing Up In Upper Canada

John A. Macdonald was born on January 11, 1815, in Glasgow, Scotland. His father, Hugh, was an intelligent and ambitious man, but he was not a successful **merchant**. There was never enough money for the family of six to live. When John was only five years old, his parents decided to sail to **Upper Canada**. This was a British **colony** in America. Here, they could make a fresh start and try to earn a better living.

The Macdonalds were a close-knit family. They settled in easily among the many other Scottish families in the Kingston area. John was a tall, handsome boy who preferred books more than athletics and liked to play imaginative games. When he played toy soldiers with his sisters, he always insisted on being the captain while they were ordinary soldiers. It was an early clue that John would grow up to be a leader.

Shortly after the family came to Canada, John's younger brother, James, died. John was the only surviving son. His parents, especially his mother, Helen, focussed their hopes and dreams on him.

John spent his early childhood in Glasgow. Some of the manors built in Glasgow at that time are still standing today.

Money was never plentiful, but John's parents found the money to pay his tuition at the best schools in the area until he was 15. Hugh and Helen ensured that John received a good education. He learned arithmetic, geography, grammar, public speaking, Latin, and Greek. John's parents wanted him to become a lawyer or a clergyman, two of the most respected professions at the time.

At the age of 15, John began work in the Kingston law office of a fellow Scot, George Mackenzie. Four years later, Macdonald had his own legal practice.

During the early 19th century, children from wealthy homes, such as Macdonald, attended school.

DEFINING MOMENT

One of Macdonald's major disappointments in life was that he was unable to attend university. He once told a fellow politician that if he had been able to attend university, he might never have entered politics and become prime minister. What he really wanted to do was study literature and become a writer.

Becoming a Politician

"You must yield to the times."

Macdonald on his political philosophy

Macdonald followed the path of many young, ambitious men in Upper Canada who wanted to become lawyers. First, he learned about law by **articling** in a law office. Later, he passed the exam that made him a lawyer. In 1835, Macdonald opened his own law firm in Kingston.

The late 1830s was a time of major political change in Upper Canada. The government was run by an **oligarchy** that made almost all of the decisions. In 1837, a group of more than 800 **rebels** led by William Lyon Mackenzie, tried to overthrow the government. Many people supported the rebels, but they did not agree with the rebels' use of violence as a means to overthrow the government.

A young Macdonald volunteered for active service during the rebellion to help defend Upper Canada from the rebels. Macdonald's military career, however, never progressed beyond drilling and marching, and he never engaged in active combat.

By the time Macdonald joined the **militia**, he was practicing law. He attracted public attention by taking difficult and even sensational cases. Although he lost as many cases

William Lyon Mackenzie was not well-liked by many people. His opponents called him a "muckraker" and "scandal-monger." A prominent member of the government even arranged an assassination attempt on Mackenzie that ultimately failed.

as he won, Macdonald acquired a reputation for having an active imagination and a quick wit.

Macdonald also was an active businessman. He bought and sold land in Kingston, Guelph, and Toronto. He was on the board of directors of several banks and insurance companies as well.

Macdonald was becoming better known in the local business and political community. In 1843, he ran as an **alderman** in Kingston's local government. The next year, he won a seat in the **legislative assembly** of the Province of Canada.

The Province of Canada was created in 1841, when Great Britain united Upper Canada and **Lower Canada**. Macdonald ran as a Conservative politician. He stressed his belief in the British connection, his commitment to the development of Canadian resources, and his devotion to the interests of Kingston.

Macdonald rose quickly through the ranks of the government. He became **attorney general** in 1854, and he was later co-premier with George-Étienne Cartier, a French-speaking lawyer born in Lower Canada. Their alliance was important in bringing English-speaking and French-speaking Canadians together to work toward common goals. Macdonald and Cartier were co-founders of the Conservative Party of Canada.

Macdonald successfully combined political wisdom with a talent for agreeableness. Macdonald put people at ease with his jokes and puns. He engaged people in lively conversation with his knowledge of **biographies**, histories, novels, and poetry. Early in his law career, people considered Macdonald to be a bit stand-offish, so he was advised to be less serious and more outgoing. This was good advice that helped him win elections and influence people.

Sir George-Étienne Cartier, from Antoine, Quebec, was a lawyer and politician.

MAJOR INFLUENCE

Under Macdonald, the government opened **asylums** in Toronto, Amherstburg, and Orillia. He created a home for the criminally insane in Kingston in 1858. The first reformatory for juvenile offenders began at Penetanguishene the following year. Macdonald also ensured that proper standards were created and enforced for these institutions.

Confederation: Macdonald's Greatest Achievement

In 1841, Great Britain had united Upper and Lower Canada into the United Province of Canada. By the 1860s, however, the colony was becoming difficult to govern. Petty jealousies, personality conflicts, and religious and cultural differences made it impossible for any one political party to gain a majority of the seats in the assembly.

George Brown was Macdonald's main opponent on the issue of Confederation. Brown was the leader of the Reform Party. He wanted Upper Canada to separate from Lower Canada. Macdonald's Conservative Party wanted to work together with the French-Canadians of Lower Canada.

In contrast, George-Étienne Cartier, a member of the Bleu Party in Lower Canada, worked well with Macdonald. Cartier believed co-operation was necessary for the survival of French-Canadian culture.

In 1886, a meeting was held in London, England to lay some of the groundwork for the British North America Act.

Antoine-Aimé Dorion's Rouge Party had completely different goals than the Reform and Conservative Parties. The Rouge Party believed strongly in French-Canadian rights. The Party wanted to end the colony's connection with Great Britain.

Between 1857 and 1864, there were three elections and five different governments. The four parties were too divided to agree on policies. As a result, few laws were passed. It was political **deadlock**.

On June 14, 1864, George Brown stood up in the assembly and announced that he was ready to accept any solution to solve the political deadlock. Brown declared, "I desire no greater honour for my children, than that I had a hand, however humble, in bringing about a solution to our difficulties."

The members of the assembly stood and cheered. Soon after, Brown, Macdonald, and Cartier joined forces in the "Great Coalition of 1864" to bring about Confederation.

The Great Coalition's plan was to separate the United Province of Canada into two provinces, Ontario and Quebec, and add the four Atlantic colonies. Each province would have its own government for local matters. A House of Commons in Ottawa would make national decisions on matters affecting more than one province. Each province would elect members to the House of Commons according to the size of its population. First, however, Canadians would have to convince the Atlantic colonies to join Canada.

The Coalition's first task was to persuade the Atlantic colonies that Confederation was a good idea. Nova Scotia, New Brunswick, and Prince Edward Island had been debating the possibility

> **"Instead of looking upon us as a merely dependent colony, England will have in us a friendly nation— a subordinate but still a powerful people— to stand by her in North America in peace and war."**
> *Macdonald*

of their own union. The Canadians asked to be invited to the Atlantic provinces' next meeting in Charlottetown on September 1, 1864. The course of Canadian history was about to change.

Vigorous and passionate speeches from John A. Macdonald, George-Étienne Cartier, and George Brown convinced the Maritime representatives that Confederation could be a positive union. They agreed to meet again in Quebec City to hammer out a new constitution.

Thirty-three delegates, including two members from Newfoundland, attended the conference at Quebec City in October 1864. Unlike the friendly mood at Charlottetown, arguments raged back and forth. However, when discussions became heated, Macdonald was often able to cool down tempers.

Constitution-making was serious business. Many important decisions needed to be made and problems had to be overcome. After 17 days of heated debate, the delegates drew up a list of 72 recommendations. They returned home to convince their governments to accept these resolutions. The politicians in Nova Scotia and New Brunswick agreed. However, Newfoundland and Prince Edward Island decided not to join Confederation.

Canada became the first **dominion** in the British Empire on July 1, 1867. A newly-knighted Sir John A. Macdonald walked to the Parliament buildings in Ottawa to become Canada's first prime minister.

Campaigns

> "I thought there was no end, nothing worthy of ambition, but now I see something which is well worthy of all I have suffered in the cause of my little country."
>
> *Macdonald on Confederation*

On November 7, 1885, the final spike was driven into the CPR at Craigellachie, British Columbia, joining the eastern and western portions of Canada.

After Confederation in 1867, the **governor general**, a representative of the Queen, **appointed** Macdonald as Canada's first prime minister. Later that year, Macdonald led the Conservative Party to a victory in Canada's first federal election. In the next few years, Macdonald brought Manitoba (1870), British Columbia (1871), and Prince Edward Island (1873) into Confederation.

The Conservatives stayed in power under Macdonald's leadership until 1873, when the Pacific Scandal occurred. The Conservatives needed money for an election campaign and accepted funds from Hugh Allan, the man whose company was trying to obtain the contract to build a transcontinental railway across Canada. The Liberals howled that accepting this money was a bribe. They claimed that Macdonald's Conservative government planned to give Allan the railway contract in exchange for money to run their campaign. The Liberals made public a telegram from Macdonald to Allan's legal adviser, John J.C. Abbott, that said, "I must have another ten thousand: will be the last time of calling: do not fail me: answer today."

Macdonald and Cartier were guilty of accepting large sums of money in exchange for government contracts. Macdonald had no choice but to resign. In the 1874 election, the Liberal Party, led by Alexander Mackenzie, swept into power.

Macdonald offered his resignation as party leader. It was rejected. During the 1878 election, he and Agnes campaigned hard. They met with many Canadians at political picnics in small towns and villages. He appealed to Canadians' sense of independence and promised to pass a "National Policy" with protective **tariffs** on manufactured goods that were imported from other countries. The tariffs would make foreign products more expensive to buy than Canadian products. The National Policy also included completing the transcontinental railway and settling the West.

At the time, Canada was suffering from an **economic depression**. The voters chose not to re-elect Alexander Mackenzie. Instead, Macdonald took the reins of the government once again. He went on to win elections in 1882 and 1887 as well.

In 1891, Macdonald ran in his last election campaign. The Liberals, under Wilfrid Laurier, wanted to bring in new policies that would closely link Canada and the United States in terms of trade.

Macdonald made many speeches against letting the United States have any part in Canadian affairs. He knew that some American politicians were talking about **annexing** Canada. Macdonald appealed to the people of Canada to support his vision of a unified and independent country. "I am a British subject and British born, and a British subject I hope to die," he declared. Macdonald said that Laurier's plans were those of a **traitor**. Macdonald won the election. He remained prime minister until his death on June 6, 1891.

PARTICIPATING POLITICS

At Confederation, many people believed that the right to vote had to be earned. Others felt that every man was born with the right to vote. Most people believed that any person who had a stake in the well-being of the community should be able to vote. This included men over 21 years of age who paid taxes, owned land, or paid a certain amount of rent. Male property owners were the only Canadians allowed to vote in 1867. They represented about 11 percent of the population.

In early Canadian history, elections provided great entertainment and continued for several days. Wooden platforms were built in the largest villages, and voters climbed onto the platform and voted by shouting the name of the man they supported. Candidates attempted to bribe voters with whisky. Heated discussions ended in fights. In 1874, the secret ballot was introduced, which made bribery more difficult.

Special People in Macdonald's Life

Sir John A. Macdonald made many financial sacrifices for his political career. Friends provided aid during times of need.

Macdonald worked hard as a lawyer. In 1842, he became very tired and ill from the long hours he worked at his office. A doctor suggested Macdonald take time away from work. He decided to visit Scotland. There, he met his cousin Isabella. They had many common interests, such as reading and learning new things. Isabella travelled to Canada the following year, and they married.

John and Isabella had two children. Their first born, John Alexander, died when he was only one year old. Macdonald never got over his son's death. He kept a box of his child's toys up until his own death.

Although the Macdonalds had a happy marriage at first, Isabella gradually became very ill, and spent most of her time sick in bed. Macdonald took her to the best doctors in Canada and the United States. However, they could not help her.

The Macdonald's second son, Hugh, was raised by his grandmother, Helen, and John's sisters. Isabella was too sick to care for Hugh, and John was away from Kingston working as a politician.

This was a difficult time for Macdonald. He worried constantly about Isabella. He also had financial difficulties. He spent so much time on his political career that he did not have enough time to work as a lawyer. As the prime minister of Canada, Macdonald earned about $5,000 a year. His legal practice brought in another $1,000 to $3,000.

Several times, Macdonald's friends came to his rescue. When he had **gallstones** in 1870, a friend discovered that the prime minister was almost broke. The friend thought it unfair that Macdonald had become poor in the service of Canada. Within two years, the friend raised $67,000 for the prime minister.

Isabella died in 1857. Ten years later, John A., as most people called him, married again. His new wife, Agnes, was very interested in politics and eager to learn about the world. She sat in the visitors' gallery of the House of Commons and sent messages to her husband via sign language.

In 1869, Agnes and John A. had a daughter named Mary. Mary was never able to walk or talk properly. John A. often returned late at night from work to hold and rock Mary to sleep. With her parents' help, Mary learned to read and use a typewriter. Macdonald sent her many letters when he was away.

Macdonald's son Hugh grew up to become very successful. As an adult, Hugh moved to Manitoba and became the province's premier. In 1891, Hugh was elected a member of Parliament from Manitoba. This meant there were two Macdonalds sitting in the House of Commons.

Mary's parents taught her how to type on a typewriter and how to read documents, such as her father's letters.

Ottawa, Canada's capital, is home to the Parliament buildings.

"Often times he comes in with a very moody brow, tired and oppressed, his voice weak, his step slow, & ten minutes after he is making clever jokes & laughing like any schoolboy, with his hands in the pockets and his head thrown back."

Excerpt from Agnes Macdonald's diary, on her husband

The Creation of Manitoba

> "No matter what happens now, the rights of the Métis are assured by the Manitoba Act: that is what I wanted—my mission is finished."
>
> *Louis Riél, 1870*

One of the motives behind Confederation was to expand west into the Prairies. In May 1867, the United States bought Alaska from Russia. Macdonald had to act quickly. In 1869, Canada bought all of the Hudson's Bay Company lands from the U.S. border north to the Arctic Ocean, and from Ontario west to the Rocky Mountains. The country could now expand west to the Pacific Ocean. However, the government did not inform the people who lived in the area about the change of ownership. This contributed to the Red River Resistance.

The most populated area in the West was the Red River Settlement (present-day Winnipeg). It consisted of about 10,000 **Métis** and a few thousand Europeans. The Métis were the offspring of European fur traders and Aboriginal women. The Métis had established a distinct culture. Many Métis spoke French, as well as Michif, a Cree dialect.

The Métis had small farms along the banks of the Red and Assiniboine Rivers. Twice a year, they followed the herds of buffalo. The buffalo hunt was central to the Métis way of life. When word spread that their land had been sold to Canada, the Métis became worried. They wondered if the new settlers would respect their rights and if their language and religious rights would be protected. The sudden appearance of a Canadian survey party in the summer of 1869 increased the fears of the Métis. The surveyors began dividing the land into large squares, as in Ontario. The Métis, however, divided their land into long, narrow strips, as in Quebec. The Métis did not want to lose their land. Louis Riél, one of the Métis, told the surveyors that they had to

MANITOBA

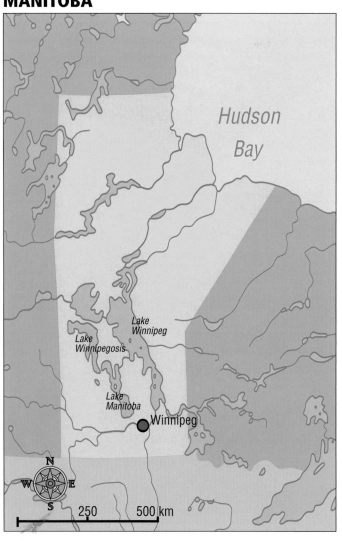

The name "Manitoba" may have come from the Cree words *manitou* (Great Spirit) and *wapow* (narrows). The Cree believed the eerie sound made by the wind and waves from Lake Manitoba crashing into Manitou Island was the voice or drumbeat of the *manitou*.

leave. Standing on the survey chain that surveyors use to measure land distance, Riél announced firmly, "You go no farther." The Canadians left, and Louis Riél became the leader of the Métis resistance, a group that refused to accept the sovereignty of the Canadian government.

Later, Riél and 400 supporters captured Fort Garry in Manitoba by force and set up a new provincial government in defiance of the Canadian government's claims on Métis land. The Métis created a list of demands, including the entry of their territory into Confederation and recognition of their land claims and way of life. The Métis sent three men to Ottawa to negotiate with Macdonald.

In the meantime, Riél had Thomas Scott, a member of a small Anglophone group, which promoted the annexation of Red River to Canada, executed for resisting the new Métis government. News of Scott's death caused a national uproar. Scott was a Protestant and from Ontario. Ontario Protestants called Riél a traitor and a murderer. They demanded that Macdonald punish him. French-Canadians considered Riél a hero, a defender of French-Canadian and Catholic rights. The country was divided on the subject. Riél was exiled to the United States.

To satisfy the Métis, Macdonald agreed to their demands. On July 15, 1870, Métis territory became the new province of Manitoba. As in Quebec, French and English received equal status as official languages. Catholics and Protestants were also given the right to established their own school systems and receive government funding.

The loss of Métis land would mean the Métis could no longer hunt buffalo, which they used for food and clothing.

Law and Order:
The North-West Mounted Police

Macdonald created the North-West Mounted Police (NWMP) in 1873. Their job was to help Aboriginal Peoples and settlers, and maintain law and order in the West. Officers wore scarlet tunics in honour of British soldiers .

In order to join the force, men had to be at least 183 centimetres tall, between 18 and 40 years of age, healthy, able to ride a horse, able to read and write in English or French, and have a good character.

About 400 men were trained in Winnipeg. In 1874, they took part in the "Great March," a patrol on horseback to the Canadian West. These men were to police 6 million kilometres of land.

The NWMP had an immediate impact. One First Nations chief on the Prairies declared, "I can sleep now safely. Before the arrival of the Police, when I laid my head down at night, every sound frightened me. My sleep was broken. Now I can sleep sound and am not afraid." The NWMP soon developed a reputation for being courageous and honest. Today, this force is called the Royal Canadian Mounted Police.

Created in 1873, the North-West Mounted Police hired men who demonstrated good character and horsemanship.

Aboriginal Issues

Macdonald had to ensure that the Aboriginal Peoples on the Prairies would allow settlers to move west. At this time, the U.S. plains were the site of fierce wars between Aboriginal Peoples and U.S. settlers. Macdonald wanted to avoid such a situation in Canada.

Aboriginal Peoples did not want to give up their lands. A Cree chief, Sweet Grass, stated, "We heard our land was sold and we did not like it. We don't want to sell our land; it is our property, and no one had a right to sell it."

Despite their concerns, Aboriginal Peoples living on the Prairies finally agreed to allow settlers to enter the West if the government would sign treaties. Aboriginal Peoples wanted the government to recognize their title to the land and to help them adjust to a new way of life. Between 1871 and 1877, Ottawa signed a series of treaties with the Plains Peoples. In return for surrendering their lands, Ottawa promised the Plains People a small amount of money each year, roughly $5 to $12 per person, a piece of land or reserve, farm animals, agricultural equipment, medical help, schools, hunting supplies, and help in times of famine.

The 1870s was a decade of disaster for Aboriginal Peoples in the West. A smallpox epidemic in 1870 killed hundreds of people. Measles, tuberculosis, and other diseases brought by settlers claimed even more lives. However, nothing could compare to the overhunting of the buffalo. The Plains peoples depended upon the buffalo as their main source of food, clothing, and tools. Repeating rifles, which did not have to be reloaded after every shot, allowed hunters to kill hundreds of animals in one hunt.

When the buffalo disappeared, the Plains peoples lost their means of livelihood. They were forced to give up their traditional way of life and learn how to till the soil and raise livestock. Between 1880 and 1885, the number of Aboriginal Peoples on the Prairies declined from 32,000 to 20,000.

With an increased European presence, the buffalo were hunted nearly to extinction, impacting both the prairie ecosystem and Aboriginal way of life.

"Where are the buffalo? Where are our horses? They are gone, and we must soon follow them. These prairies were ours once, and the buffalo were given to us by the Great Spirit….But they are all gone…. Let them send the buffalo back. Give us the prairies again and we won't ask for food. But it is too late. It is too late."

Cree leader on the overhunting of the buffalo

French-Canadian Resistance

> "Fifteen years ago, I gave my heart to my nation. I am ready to give it again."
>
> *Riél after being invited by the Métis to return to Canada*

In the late 1800s, settlers from Canada began to move west of Manitoba. Their presence awakened Métis fears. When the Canadian government began to survey the land, tension increased in every Métis community. The Métis held mass meetings. They sent many petitions to Macdonald requesting rights of possession to their farms. Macdonald did not respond.

In 1884, the Métis invited Louis Riél to return to Canada from exile in the United States. Riél had been successful in getting Macdonald to agree to Métis requests in 1869. The Métis hoped he could repeat this success in 1884.

Riél was greeted as a hero. He dreamed of creating a new church in which the Métis were the chosen people and he was their prophet.

Riél decided to use the same tactics that had been successful in 1869. On March 19, he created a temporary government. He hoped that Macdonald would negotiate with the Métis as he had done in 1870. "The time had now come," Riél declared, "to rule this country or perish in the attempt."

Fighting began one week later when a NWMP patrol marched out to arrest Riél. At Duck Lake the patrol met and fought a group of armed Métis.

Louis Riél was born on the Red River Settlement in 1844. Riél could speak English, French, and Cree.

Within 10 days of the Duck Lake battle, the Canadian government raised 5,000 volunteer soldiers. The Métis were no match for the well-armed soldiers. Riél surrendered.

During the summer of 1885, Louis Riél's trial in Regina made newspaper headlines across the country. Riél was charged with **treason**. The penalty was death. Defence lawyers argued that Riél was not guilty by virtue of insanity. However, Riél disagreed. To be judged insane would imply that the Métis did not have just causes to rebel. Riél believed they did.

The jury met for one hour before deciding that Riél was guilty. Although they recommended mercy, the judge ruled that Louis Riél "be hanged by the neck till you are dead, and may God have mercy on your soul." Thus began a heated controversy between French- and English-Canadians.

English Canadians demanded that Riél hang. They still remembered Thomas Scott's death. When many people in Ontario attacked Riél as a Roman Catholic and a French-Canadian troublemaker, Quebec took his side. French-Canadians demanded that Macdonald cancel the death sentence and place Riél in an insane asylum. Macdonald twice postponed the execution. Forced to make a decision, Macdonald decided to let Riél hang. Ontario had more votes than Quebec, and Macdonald believed Riél was guilty. Riél was hung on November 16, 1885.

In recent times, Riél has become a symbol for government resistance. Canadians have erected statues in his honour.

Thomas Scott was executed on March 4, 1870.

U.S. Issues

In 1861, a **civil war** erupted in the United States between the South and the North. The Northern United States and Great Britain almost came to the brink of war because of the civil conflict. The Northern United States stopped a British ship, the *Trent*, and imprisoned two Southern U.S. soldiers who were going to Great Britain to seek military assistance. Great Britain demanded an apology and the release of the prisoners. U.S. President, and leader of the North, Abraham Lincoln refused. For two months the British colonies feared a war in which they would be the battleground. The Trent Affair ended when Lincoln released the prisoners without an apology. It showed Canadians the danger they faced to the South.

With such a long border, and without a railway across the country to move troops quickly, Canada could be easily conquered. Confederation, Macdonald argued, would supply the money to build a railway between the provinces. George Brown stated, "The Americans are now a warlike people. They have large armies, a powerful navy, an unlimited supply of warlike munitions... unless we are willing to live at the mercy of our neighbours, we, too, must put our country in a state of efficient preparation."

In addition to the U.S. Civil war, Canadians were also concerned about the Fenians, former Irish-American soldiers who wanted Great Britain to free Ireland. The Fenians' plan was to capture Canada and trade it to Great Britain in return for Ireland's freedom. The Fenians attacked New Brunswick and several places in Canada in 1866. These raids convinced many people in New Brunswick of the need for Confederation.

During the U.S. Civil War, the North and the South collided in a battle in Williamsburg, Virginia, in 1862.

Joining Canada from Sea to Sea

Although one of the motives behind Confederation was to build a railway from sea to sea, it was not until 1880 that the government persuaded a private company to undertake the task. In return for 10 million hectares of the best land in the West plus $25 million, the CPR Company agreed to build a rail line from Ontario to the Pacific. The completed railway would be two-thirds longer than any other railway in the world.

At this time, few people had ever travelled from Ontario to the Pacific Ocean. The West had not been fully surveyed. Macdonald, however, believed that a railway was necessary to Canada's survival. The United States had bought Alaska from Russia and was interested in Canada's western lands. It was important to settle this area with Canadians.

The CPR hired William Van Horne to oversee the construction of the railway. Van Horne was a tireless worker. Often working around the clock, 5,000 men and 1,700 teams of horses laid track across the Prairies in less than two years.

The land to the north of Lake Superior consisted of granite rock, fast-flowing rivers, tall forests, and muskeg. The muskeg looked like solid ground, but it was really a layer of thick moss covering a lake of black water. The railway workers used dynamite to clear a path for the track through the rocky hills, and then they dumped the rock in the muskeg to fill the lakes. One stretch of track was swallowed by the waters of the muskeg seven consecutive times, including three locomotives before railway workers filled it with enough rock to become solid.

The Rocky Mountains presented an even greater challenge than the muskeg. In places, the route had to be blasted out of canyon walls. Workers were lowered over the cliff on ropes to drill blasting holes in the face of the mountain. They had to scramble to safety before the dynamite exploded. The line between the Pacific Ocean and Kamloops, British Columbia, required 27 tunnels and 600 **trestle** bridges.

The completion of the line in 1885 was an engineering miracle that cost many human lives. Working conditions were extremely dangerous. Dynamite exploded early. Mud and rock slides killed many people. In British Columbia, labourers from China worked for very low wages and were treated poorly by the company and their co-workers of European ancestry.

The completion of the transcontinental railway in the 1880s had a tremendous impact upon the West. For Aboriginal Peoples, it signalled the end of their traditional ways of life. The railway brought settlers to the West. The population mushroomed from 1,000 in 1870 to 50,000 a mere 20 years later. Settlements, such as Regina, Moose Jaw, Medicine Hat, and Calgary, sprang up almost overnight along the main line of the railway.

> "Next summer, or at the latest next fall, the railway will be close to us... [people of European ancestry] will fill the country and they will dictate to us as they please. It is useless to dream that we can frighten them, that time is passed."
> *Chief Poundmaker, 1885*

In the Public Eye

The 1891 election exhausted Macdonald. The campaign had been unusually difficult. "If you would know the depth of meanness of human nature," he stated, "you have got to be a Prime Minister running a general election." He died several months later on June 6, 1891.

The entire country mourned. For many Canadians, his death represented the end of an era. He had been Canada's prime minister for more than 19 years. Except for the five years after the Pacific Scandal, Macdonald had been Canada's only prime minister.

On the day of his funeral in Ottawa, there was a thunderstorm with sheets of rain. Thousands of people stood silently, heads bowed in respect as the train carrying his body puffed its way toward Kingston. He was buried in the Cataraqui Cemetery.

One time, Macdonald said, "Even my enemies will admit that I am no boaster—that there does not exist in Canada a man who has given more of his time, more of his heart, more of his wealth, or more of his intellect and power, such as they may be, for the good of this Dominion of Canada."

John A. Macdonald never retired. He died while in office.

Macdonald's Legacy

John A. Macdonald truly was the founder of Canada. He promised Canadians a united country, and he delivered.

Macdonald's greatest achievement, to that effect, was Confederation. He spearheaded discussions at conferences in Charlottetown and Quebec City. He listened carefully to French-Canadians who wanted guarantees that their language, religion, and customs would be protected. Without the agreement of French-Canadians, Confederation would never have happened.

Macdonald's dream to unite Canada from the Atlantic to the Pacific became a reality while he was in office. His government moved quickly to buy the land in the West. Under his leadership, Manitoba entered Confederation (1870), as did British Columbia (1871) and Prince Edward Island (1873). The completion of the CPR in 1885, connecting the east and west Canadian coasts further extended Macdonald's vision of a united Canada.

Macdonald believed that all Canadians should be able to enjoy the wilderness across Canada. He proposed that land be set aside. Thanks to Macdonald, there is a network of public parks across the country.

Macdonald also believed that "Canada was for Canadians." He created a national policy to protect Canadian companies by placing tariffs on imported goods. He knew that a healthy economy was necessary for the country to thrive. He felt strongly that Canadians should support and help each other.

Another legacy of the Macdonald era was the North-West Mounted Police, which Macdonald created in 1873 to bring peace and stability to the West.

In 1885, the first national park was opened at Banff, Alberta.

The Next Generation of Prime Ministers

> "The one calamity above all others which stand before this country is that political divisions should follow the division of race and the division of religion."
>
> *John Thompson*

Alexander Mackenzie

Mackenzie Bowell

Charles Tupper

John Abbott

John Thompson

In five years, four prime ministers held and lost office after John A. Macdonald died.

Macdonald's death in 1891 created a crisis for the Conservative Party. Macdonald had not prepared anyone to take his place. At 76 years old, tired and worn down, Macdonald still felt he was the best person to be prime minister.

In 1890, the year before his death, Macdonald's son Hugh wrote a letter to him about the leadership problem. In it, he said, "There is practically no Conservative Party in Canada at the present time. There is a very strong 'John A' Party." Hugh looked ahead to the future and told his father, "I fear a process of rapid disintegration will set in, when anyone else attempts to take command." Hugh was right. In the five years after Macdonald's death, there were four Conservative prime ministers.

The first, John Abbott, did not not really want to be prime minister. He accepted the job because the Conservative Party could not agree on another leader. He became prime minister on the condition that he could remain in the **Senate**. This condition worked in theory, however, it did not work in practice. Only persons elected to the House of Commons are allowed to speak there, which meant Abbott needed other Conservative representatives to speak for him in Parliament on a daily basis.

The next prime minister, John Thompson, was a respected judge. He was particularly interested in criminal law and believed that the punishment should be appropriate to the crime and situation.

He ran the everyday government affairs in the House of Commons on John Abbott's behalf. Abbott resigned due to ill health, and Thompson became the prime minister. When Thompson died in office, Mackenzie Bowell became prime minister. Bowell was disliked by many members of his **cabinet**, and they forced him to resign. Charles Tupper took over as prime minister. He was a well-respected Father of Confederation from Nova Scotia. Tupper was in office only a short time before the Conservatives' five-year term ended. It was time for an election.

The Liberals, under Wilfrid Laurier, returned to power in 1896 after an 18-year absence.

Macdonald served longer as prime minister than the next five prime ministers combined.

Keeping Canada Together

"I have a long life of politics, a long life of official duties. I have committed many mistakes... I have tried according to the best of my judgement, to do what I could for the well-being of good government and the future prosperity of this my beloved country."
John A. Macdonald

Alexander Mackenzie: Canada's First Liberal Prime Minister

Alexander Mackenzie was born in Scotland on January 28, 1822. He was the third of 10 sons—three of whom died as infants.

In 1873, Mackenzie became prime minister. The Conservatives resigned because of the Pacific Railway Scandal. Governor General Lord Dufferin asked Mackenzie and the Liberal Party to form a new government. Mackenzie was a former stone mason and contractor. He believed that, in a democracy, the people should choose the government. He called a general election and was rewarded with a majority government.

It was not a good time to be prime minister. Canada, like many countries, was in the grip of an economic depression. Prices were falling for manufactured goods and natural resources, such as timber and grain.

Prime Minister Alexander Mackenzie led the first Liberal government.

> "We have a country vast in extent, vast in its territorial magnitude, vast in respect to its sectional views, and in its diversity of creed and race."
>
> *Alexander Mackenzie*

Although the economic situation was not Mackenzie's fault, he needed to improve the economy and help Canadians find and keep jobs. During the election, he promised voters he would lower tariffs on goods that were made in the United States and imported into Canada. That would make these products less expensive for Canadians to buy. After he won the election, he could not back up his promises with action. Instead, he had to raise tariffs to pay for government programs. This angered voters. They expected to save money. Now, they had to pay more at a time they were already finding it difficult to pay their bills.

Mackenzie also upset people in British Columbia. In 1871, it was the promise of the railway that had been a deciding factor in British Columbia's decision to join Confederation. Mackenzie thought building a transcontinental railway to British Columbia was too expensive, especially since there were so few people living there. He stalled construction plans. The dispute became so heated that British Colombia threatened to leave Canada. The governor general had to intervene in order to settle the dispute and continue the plans for the railway. Despite Mackenzie's objections, during his tenure as prime minister, 4,000 kilometres of railway tracks were laid.

Voters had high expectations of Canada's first Liberal government. Mackenzie was well-intentioned and honest. However, he had difficulty resolving conflicts. Macdonald and the Conservatives took advantage of this weakness and told voters they would complete the railway and return Canada to prosperity. In 1878, the Conservatives swept into power, defeating Mackenzie by a large margin.

During Mackenzie's time as prime minister, his government established the **Supreme Court of Canada**. It introduced the secret ballot and the requirement that elections be held in one day.

The Liberals passed the Post Office Act of 1875. This act created door-to-door mail delivery in all major Canadian cities. The Northwest Territories Act of 1875 provided the Northwest Territories with a constitution.

Alexander Mackenzie died on April 17, 1892. He had been bedridden after a fall near his home. He did not have a state funeral. Many people came to pay their respects at services in Toronto and Sarnia.

FREE TRADE

Since the 1800s, the idea of free trade with the United States has appealed to some Canadians and angered others. Those who supported free trade argued that it would create jobs in Canada and be good for the economy. Other people opposed free trade on the grounds that it would be the first step towards Canada becoming part of the United States. Canada signed a limited free trade agreement with the United States in 1849, which lasted until 1866. In the 1887 and 1891 elections, the Liberal Party promised to pass free trade. Despite this promise, or perhaps because of it, Canadian voters elected Macdonald and the Conservative Party.

John Abbott: The Country's First Canadian-born Prime Minister

John Abbott married Mary Bethune in 1849. They had four sons and four daughters.

John Joseph Caldwell Abbott was born in St. Andrews, Quebec, in 1821. He was educated by his father, an Anglican missionary. At 17 years of age, Abbott began work in the clothing business, where he learned accounting and bookkeeping.

In 1843, Abbott started law school at the University of McGill. He became a lawyer in 1847. Later, he taught law at McGill. One of his students was future Prime Minister Wilfrid Laurier.

Abbott was also a businessman. He owned shares in several Montreal companies and was company president of Canada Central Railway, a key link in the transcontinental line. From 1887 to 1888, Abbott was mayor of Montreal.

Although Abbott did many different things, his most notable position was as prime minster. He had several firsts in the role, including being the first Canadian prime minister to be born on Canadian soil. He was the first Senator to become prime minister of Canada. He was also the first prime minister to be a member of both the House of Commons and the Senate.

"I hate politics, and what are considered their appropriate methods. I hate notoriety, public meetings, public speeches, caucuses, and everything that I know of that is apparently the necessary incident of politics—except doing public work to the best of my ability."
John Abbott, June 4, 1891

Abbott was not the Conservative Party's first choice to be its leader. Charles Tupper, a cabinet minister for Macdonald, was. However, the governor general at the time did not like Tupper, so the Conservatives decided not to elect him as Party leader.

A highly regarded and wealthy lawyer whose clients included some of the country's largest companies, Abbott was a senator when Macdonald died. He had been a member of Parliament as well. Abbott thought John Thompson, the energetic and brilliant Minister of Justice, would make a better prime minister. Thompson, however, was a Roman Catholic. Although he was respected by many Protestants,

some people did not want a man of his religion to lead the country. Abbott was the compromise. Abbott agreed to become prime minister as long as he could stay in the Senate.

One of the positive measures Abbott implemented, that he is perhaps best known for, was reforming the civil service so people were hired for their abilities and not their political connections.

When Abbott's health failed in 1892, he retired. Thompson became prime minister. Abbott was prime minister less than 18 months. He died less than a year after his retirement.

John Abbott supported the construction of a transcontinental railway.

RAILWAY MAN

John Abbott was a man of many interests. He cultivated orchids, took singing lessons, and was a railway fanatic. His father shared this passion, and his younger brother was a well-known railway engineer. The family invested money in local railways. Abbott was also at the heart of the Pacific Scandal. He was a Conservative member of Parliament and, at the same time, the lawyer for Hugh Allan, president of the CPR. Allan made donations to the Conservative Party in exchange for a contract to build the transcontinental railway.

John Thompson: Justice Was His Passion

John Thompson wrote love notes to his future wife, Annie, in shorthand, so Annie's parents would not be able to understand the letters.

John Sparrow David Thompson was born November 10, 1845, in Halifax, Nova Scotia. A year after marrying Annie, a Roman Catholic, Thompson announced that he had converted to Roman Catholicism. At the time, Catholics and Protestants did not get along. Thompson believed that converting to Catholicism ended his chances of professional success as a lawyer. However, Thompson's Protestant clients continued to use his services.

Thompson was the popular choice among the Conservatives to replace John A. Macdonald. Experienced and very honest, Thompson was a former member of the Nova Scotia Legislative Assembly. He also was the province's **premier** for a short time. Thompson left politics to become a judge in the Nova Scotia Supreme Court. His personal philosophy was that people should "play fair."

Macdonald convinced Thompson to return to politics in 1885. Macdonald was 70 years old, and the strain of so many years in politics was taking its toll on him. Many of Macdonald's cabinet ministers were retiring or had died. He needed younger, talented men like 40-year-old Thompson to work with him. Thompson acted as Macdonald's unofficial second-in-command.

Although Abbott was chosen to replace Macdonald in 1891 over Thompson because of Thompson's religious beliefs, Abbott did not stay in office long. On December 5, 1892, Thompson was elected prime minister. He gave his first major speech as prime minister in January 1893. It was about tolerance and Canadian **nationalism**.

Thompson was a passionate nationalist, but he believed Canada needed British protection from the United States. He thought that complete independence would have to wait until Canada had a population of 50 million.

Thompson's major concern in 1893 and 1894 was the Northwest Territories schools question. Roman Catholics wanted separate schools supported by government funds. Many Protestants did not want to provide public funding for Catholic schools.

Thompson went to London at the end of October 1894 to be knighted by Queen Victoria and to consult doctors about his poor health. Shortly after he sat down to lunch at Windsor Castle, he suffered a heart attack and died.

Thompson's major contribution to Canada was the creation of the **Criminal Code**. He allowed suspects to testify on their own behalf and punishments for juveniles to be lightened.

> **"The greatest discovery of my life was my discovery of Thompson."**
> *John A. Macdonald*

WOMEN'S RIGHTS

John Thompson valued the views of women and expected that women would soon be allowed to vote. In 1893 he said: "The Conservative Party believes that the influence of women in the politics of the country is always for good. I think, therefore, that there is a probability of the franchise being extended to the women on the same property qualifications as men." However, women in Canada were first allowed to vote in federal elections in 1918.

Windsor Castle, where Thompson died, was one of Queen Victoria's official residences.

Mackenzie Bowell: Forced to Resign

Mackenzie Bowell served as both minister of customs and minister of commerce before becoming prime minister.

The sudden death of John Thompson resulted in a scurry of activity to find a prime minister. In 1894, Mackenzie Bowell became Canada's fifth prime minister.

Bowell was eager to be prime minister. He had seen Macdonald's methods of governing the party, and he believed he could copy them.

Mackenzie Bowell was born in England on December 27, 1824. He came to Canada with his parents in 1833.

First elected to the House of Commons in 1867, Bowell was the publisher of the *Belleville Intelligencer* daily newspaper. His love of politics drove him to seek a seat in Parliament at the time of Confederation. Bowell served Macdonald loyally as minister of customs—the department that oversaw the collection of tariffs—and later as minister of commerce.

As prime minister, Bowell could not cope with the controversy known as the Manitoba schools question. Similar to the Northwest Territories schools question, the issue was whether Manitoba Catholic schools should be funded by the government. Protestants and Catholics, French-speaking and English-speaking people, all had different views. Even in his own cabinet, Bowell was unable to get everyone to agree on a course of action. He was not a natural-born leader like John A. Macdonald. Further complicating his problems, Bowell was a senator, not an elected member of Parliament. He could not speak in the House of Commons. He had to watch from the sidelines as other politicians debated the issue.

The Manitoba schools question divided the Conservative Party. Charles Tupper angrily told Bowell, "You cannot, I fear, keep Parliament together long enough to see the end of this fire." Finally, seven cabinet members resigned in order to force Bowell to step down as prime minister. The day-to-day business of the government ground to a halt. After four days, Bowell admitted that he could not find enough supporters to form the government.

The governor general intervened, and 10 days later, six ministers were reinstated. At this time

Charles Tupper joined the cabinet. Although the governor general attempted to help Bowell keep his position as prime minister, Tupper took virtual control over the Conservative Party and became the next prime minister. In 1917, Bowell died of old age at his home in Belleville.

CANADA LINKED TO THE WORLD

Bowell represented Canada at a trade conference of British colonies in Australia in 1887. One of the proposals at the conference was to construct an underwater telegraph cable between North America and Australia. It was built in 1902 and connected British Columbia to Australia.

The trans-Pacific cable spans nearly 6,500 kilometres from the Bamfield cable station in British Columbia to Fanning Island, Fiji, New Zealand, and Australia.

Charles Tupper: The Time Was Not Right

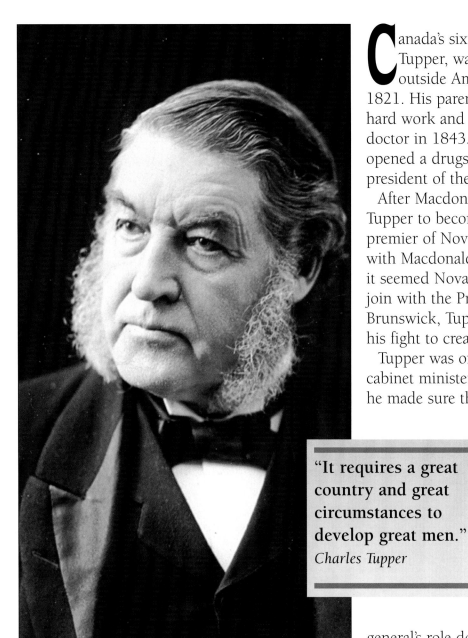

Tupper was born in Amherst, Nova Scotia. When he died, he was buried in Halifax, Nova Scotia.

> "It requires a great country and great circumstances to develop great men."
> *Charles Tupper*

anada's sixth prime minister, Charles Tupper, was born on his father's farm outside Amherst, Nova Scotia, on July 2, 1821. His parents taught him the benefits of hard work and self-discipline. Tupper became a doctor in 1843. He established a practice and opened a drugstore in Amherst. Later, he was president of the Canadian Medical Association.

After Macdonald died, there was support for Tupper to become prime minister. A former premier of Nova Scotia, Tupper had worked with Macdonald since the 1860s. Even when it seemed Nova Scotia might decide not to join with the Province of Canada and New Brunswick, Tupper had stayed steadfast in his fight to create a united Canada.

Tupper was one of Macdonald's most trusted cabinet ministers. As Minister of Public Works, he made sure the transcontinental railway was built. His efforts to rebuild the Conservative Party after the Pacific Scandal resulted in the Conservatives' return to power.

However, there was a roadblock in Tupper's path. In those days, the governor general had some say as to who would become prime minister. Today, the governor general's role does not have the same power. Governor General Lord Aberdeen discouraged the Conservatives from selecting Tupper as prime minister. Instead, Abbott became prime minister.

As it became clear that Bowell could not solve the conflict within the Conservative Party over the Manitoba schools question, the pressure for Tupper's return mounted. On January 4, 1896, seven members of the cabinet forced Bowell and the governor general to agree that Tupper would become prime minister when Bowell resigned.

On the critical issue of separate schools in Manitoba, Tupper never wavered. Although personally opposed to funding separate schools, he believed a promise had been made to the Catholic minority to have their schools funded by government money.

Tupper fought hard during the 1896 election. Although the Conservatives won more votes than the Liberals, it was the Liberal landslide in Quebec that gave Laurier a majority vote and returned the Liberals to power.

After losing in the 1900 election, Tupper resigned as party leader. He selected a fellow Nova Scotian and friend, Robert Laird Borden, to succeed him. Although Tupper's health declined, at age 84, on a visit to Rome, he had enough energy to begin the study of Italian. On October 30, 1915, the last of the original **Fathers of Confederation** died. He was buried beside his wife in Halifax. The state funeral procession stretched for more than one-and-a-half kilometres.

TUPPER TRIVIA

Tupper holds a number of records.

- His term as prime minister was the shortest in history—only 69 days.

- He was the longest-married prime minister— 65 years.

- He was the oldest person to assume the prime ministership—74 years and 10 months.

- He was a cabinet minister in the governments of four prime ministers: Macdonald, Abbott, Thompson, and Bowell.

NOVA SCOTIA

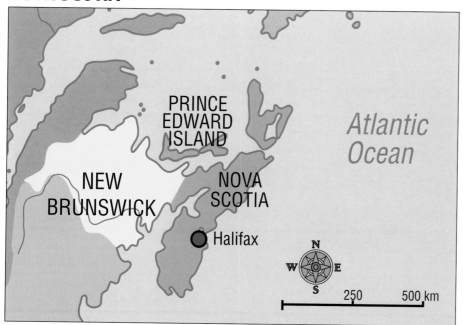

"No intelligent man... can feel for a moment that, as a Canadian, he does not occupy a far higher status than he ever could have done as a New Brunswicker, a Prince Edward Islander, or a Nova Scotian."
Charles Tupper

Timeline

1830s	1840s	1850s	1860s

PRIME MINISTERS

Macdonald becomes a lawyer and begins a practice in Kingston in 1834. 	Macdonald marries his first wife Isabella in 1843. She dies in 1857. Macdonald is elected as a member of the Legislative Assembly of the Province of Canada in 1844.	Macdonald becomes co-premier of the Province of Canada with George-Étienne Cartier in 1858.	Macdonald marries Agnes in February 1867. Their daughter Mary is born in 1869. Queen Victoria knights Macdonald for his role in Confederation in 1867.

CANADA

Rebellions break out against British authority in the colonies of Upper and Lower Canada in 1837.	The Act of Union joins Upper Canada and Lower Canada to create the United Province of Canada in 1841.	The first Canadian passenger train travels from Montreal to Toronto in 1856.	The British North America Act joins together Nova Scotia, the United Province of Canada, and New Brunswick into the **Dominion of Canada** on July 1, 1867. Louis Riél leads the Métis in the Red River Resistance in 1869.

WORLD

Victoria, at 18, becomes Queen of England in 1837. She and her husband, Prince Albert, have 9 children.	Great Britain and the United States settle Canada's borders under the Webster-Ashburton Treaty in 1842.	In 1851, the first large-scale commercial ice cream plant was established by Jacob Fussell in the United States. 	United States fights a Civil War, 1861–1865.

1870s   1880s   1890s

PRIME MINISTERS

Macdonald creates the North-West Mounted Police in 1873.

In 1885, the last spike of the CPR is driven into the ground, completing the railroad and uniting the provinces from the Atlantic to the Pacific Ocean.

In 1891, Macdonald runs in his last election campaign. His government is re-elected, but he dies several months later.

CANADA

More provinces join Confederation: Manitoba in 1870, British Columbia in 1871, and Prince Edward Island in 1873. In 1874, Macdonald's Conservatives lose the election because of the Pacific Scandal.

Louis Riél, leader of the Métis Resistance, is captured and executed by the Canadian government in 1885.

Between 1891 and 1896, four Conservative prime ministers succeed Macdonald. Wilfrid Laurier's Liberals win the election and stay in power from 1896–1911.

WORLD

In 1874, Alexander Graham Bell begins work on his new invention, the telephone, in Brantford, Ontario.

Twenty-four countries agree to the idea of Standard Time as proposed by Sandford Fleming. It divides the world into 24 equal time zones.

In 1895, Auguste and Louis Lumière were the first to show a motion picture to a paying audience of more than one person. Louis thought movies would never become popular, "Cinema is an invention without a future."

Did You Know?

Although most nations' leaders must be born in the country they are leading, Canada allows any Canadian, no matter where he or she was the born, the opportunity to run for office.

The queen of England knighted seven of the first eight prime ministers. Alexander Mackenzie did not accept a knighthood from Queen Victoria. He thought all Canadians should be treated equally.

Although representatives of the British colony of Newfoundland were at the Quebec Conference in 1864 as observers, Newfoundland did not join Confederation in 1867. In 1949, Newfoundland became the last province to join Canada.

Prime Minister Alexander Mackenzie trained as a stone mason and owned a large construction company that built many prestigious buildings. When he worked on plans for the Parliament buildings, he included a secret escape hatch in the form of a circular staircase leading directly from his office to the outside of the building.

In 1916, the Parliament buildings burned to the ground in an accidental fire. Parliament was rebuilt by John Pearson and Jean Omer Marchand.

Test Your Knowledge

Question:

How many children did Macdonald have?

three

Question:

In what year did Confederation take place?

1867

Multiple:

Who was the leader of the Métis resistance?

A) Thomas Scott
B) Louis Riél
C) David Thompson

B) Louis Riél

Question:

Who was the first Liberal prime minister of Canada?

Alexander Mackenzie

Question:

When Macdonald played toy soldiers with his sisters, what role did he always want?

captain

Question:

Macdonald created the first national park. Where is it located?

Banff, Alberta

Multiple:

Which animal provided Aboriginal Peoples of the Prairies with most of their needs?

A) beaver
B) caribou
C) buffalo

C) buffalo

Multiple:

Who was Canada's first prime minister?

A) John A. Macdonald
B) Wilfrid Laurier
C) John Abbott

A) John A. Macdonald

Question:

What is the name today of the North-West Mounted Police?

the Royal Canadian Mounted Police

Activity

When people debate a topic, two sides take a different viewpoint about one idea. They present logical arguments to support their views. Usually, each person or team is given a set amount of time to present its case. The presenters take turns stating their arguments until the total time set aside for the debate is used up. Sometimes there is an audience in the room listening to the presentations. Later, the members of the audience vote for the person or team they think made the most persuasive arguments.

Debating is an important skill. It helps people to think about ideas thoughtfully and carefully. It also helps them develop rhythms of speech that others can follow easily. John A. Macdonald learned to debate in school. He later said that debating taught him how to present his ideas strongly in Parliament so that politicians who at first did not agree with him became convinced he was right.

Some schools have organized debating clubs as part of their after-school activities. Schools often hold debates in their history class or as part of studying about world events.

A TOPIC ABOUT CANADIAN PRIME MINISTERS FOR CLASSROOM DEBATE

Many countries have a special celebration day each year to honour the leaders of their country. In the United States, for example, on the third Monday in February, Americans celebrate Presidents' Day to honour present and all of the past presidents of that country.

Canada does not have a Prime Ministers' Day. Do you think we should create a public holiday to remember Sir John A. Macdonald and all of the other prime ministers for their contribution to Canada?

Further Research

Books

To find out more about Canadian prime ministers, visit your local library. Most libraries have computers that connect to a database for researching information. If you input a key word, you will be provided with a list of books in the library that contain information on that topic. Non-fiction books are arranged numerically, using their call number. Fiction books are organized alphabetically by the author's last name.

Websites

The World Wide Web is also a good source of information. Reputable websites usually include government sites, educational sites, and online encyclopedias. Visit the following sites to learn more about Canadian prime ministers.

Learn about the lives and accomplishments of Canadian prime ministers.
www.collectionscanada.ca/primeministers/index-e.html

Check out this special Confederation website just for kids.
www.collectionscanada.ca/confederation/kids/index-e.html

The Canadian Encyclopedia Online is an excellent source of all things Canadian.
www.thecanadianencyclopedia.com

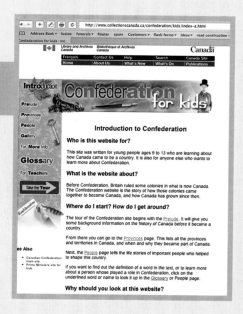

Glossary

annexing: to incorporate into a country the territory of another country

appointed: chosen to work in an office or a position

articling: studying with a lawyer to learn the profession

asylums: places where the mentally ill were once housed

attorney general: the chief law officer of Canada

biographies: written stories of people's lives

civil war: a war between citizens of the same country

deadlock: a position in which it is impossible to act or continue because of disagreement

economic depression: a time period of high unemployment and low sales of products

gallstones: a pebble-like mass that can form in the gall bladder or its duct and result in a painful illness

merchant: a personal who buys and sells items to make a profit

Métis: a person whose ancestors were both European and Aboriginal

militia: part of an army made up of civilians who undergo training for emergency duty

nationalism: patriotic feelings or efforts

rebels: people who revolt against the government

tariffs: taxes on imported goods

traitor: a person who betrays his or her country or ruler

treason: the act of betraying one's country or ruler

trestle: a framework used as a bridge to support a road or railway tracks

Political Terms

alderman: a member of the city government, who is elected by the people of a certain area

attorney general: the chief law officer of Canada

cabinet: elected members of Parliament chosen by the prime minister to be responsible for specific areas, for example, health or aboriginal affairs

civil service: people who work for the administration of the government

colony: a region ruled by a country that is usually far away

Confederation: the event in 1867 when Canada became its own country; the original four provinces were Quebec, Ontario, Nova Scotia, and New Brunswick

Criminal Code: a group of government laws about justice, crime, and punishment

dominion: certain self-governing countries in the Commonwealth, such as Canada

Dominion of Canada: a self-governing nation created in 1867 by the British North America Act that included Ontario, Quebec, Nova Scotia, and New Brunswick

Fathers of Confederation: political leaders from the British North American colonies responsible for Confederation

governor general: the representative of the British monarch in Canada

House of Commons: people who have been elected from across Canada to make laws for the entire country

legislative assembly: the elected body in the various colonies of British North America

Lower Canada: a mostly French-speaking colony created by Great Britain in 1791, re-named Canada East in 1841 when it united with Upper Canada, or Canada West, to form the United Province of Canada; today, Lower Canada is known as Quebec

oligarchy: a form of government in which only a few people have power

Parliament: the House of Commons and the Senate

premier: a Canadian province's head of government

Senate: a group of people made up of representatives from each province who review laws passed by the House of Commons

Supreme Court of Canada: the highest court in Canada

Upper Canada: mostly English-speaking colony created by Great Britain in 1791, re-named Canada West in 1841 when it united with Lower Canada (Canada East) to form the United Province of Canada. Today, Upper Canada is known as Ontario.

Index